ASPECTS OF BRITISH BLACK HISTORY

Peter Fryer

Index I
Lond

Copyright 1993 Peter Fryer

Published by Index Books (Indexreach) Ltd.
28 Charlotte Streeet, London W1P 1HJ

Typeset by Sumner Type, London
Printed by Trade Union Printing Services, Newcastle upon Tyne

A C.I.P. catalogue record for this book is available from the British Library

ISBN 1-871518-04-0

CONTENTS

Preface

This booklet is a revised and expanded version of a series of lectures given in the Conway Hall, London, in May and June 1988, under the auspices of the weekly *Workers Press*. I am grateful to the people who attended those lectures for their searching questions and thoughtful contributions to discussion. Readers of my book *Black People in the British Empire: An Introduction* (Pluto Press, 1988) will see that there is inevitably some overlap between that book and the text of the present booklet, which I hope will reach many more readers than the book has done.

P.F.

1

The politics of British black history

A white person who ventures to speak or write on any aspect of black history must first of all answer the question: 'What has black history got to do with white people?' If I don't ask this question myself and try to answer it, right at the beginning, someone is inevitably going to ask it from the floor. And rightly so.

This question comes in various forms. Sometimes it is put, not to me, but to the black people present, in some such form as this: 'Why should we listen to a white person telling us about our own history?'

Now, however it is phrased, this is a political question: I mean it's a question about power and how power is distributed or, more precisely, polarised in the society we live in. And failure to face this question, and try to answer it, suggests ignorance, incompetence, or bad faith. Some white people in Britain have much more power than is good for them, or for the rest of us. But no black person has any real power at all, even if he or she wears a police uniform or sits in parliament. The very word 'race', which geneticists and anthropologists have discarded as meaningless, survives merely as a political category. In Britain, as in South Africa, racial labels survive as devices to shut out a section of the population from power, to turn them into second-class citizens. There has been a continuous black presence in this country for something like 500 years. All that time, some white people have had all the power in their own hands and no black person has had any power at all, save of the most token kind. And white historians, almost without exception, have done their best to deprive black people of their history, too. They have consistently belittled or wiped out the black past —

which is essentially just another way of depriving black people of power. So it's hardly surprising that serious students of black history have tended to view white writers on the subject with misgivings. In the United States, some students of black history have seen its chief purpose as the encouragement of black pride and a feeling of personal worth; this is obviously not the business of white writers. Yet there are in the United States black historians who are saying, with Benjamin Quarles, doyen of African-American historians, that 'black history is no longer a matter of limited concern', that white people too need to know at least something about black history, since for them it provides 'a new version of American history, one that especially challenges our national sense of smugness and self-righteousness and our avowal of fair play'.

This statement applies with no less force to Britain and British history. Here too white people need to know something about black history, since for us it furnishes a version of British history that strongly challenges *our* national sense of smugness and self-righteousness, *our* avowal of fair play. Like American history, British history cannot be written honestly or taught honestly without taking into account the contribution that black people have made to it. In other words, without the black element, which penetrates and has been penetrated by everything else, British history is seriously and misleadingly incomplete.

In the 1980s we saw the launching of an ideological offensive by the Thatcher government in the area of history teaching. Thatcher and her friends were displeased, even alarmed, by the amount of people's history, or radical history, or history from below — call it what you will — that was allegedly being taught in our schools. They wanted the history taught in our schools to project what *The Times Higher Education Supplement* (2 September 1983) called 'an interpretation of the British experience that is expedient to our present leaders rather than faithful to the historical record'. They wanted school history to be 'patriotic' history. They wanted to return to the days when British history was a chronicle of kings and queens, national saviours, heroes and heroines, great leaders in peace and war — to the days when, as a matter of course, British history was taught in British schools as drum-and-trumpet history. In the words of Sir John Stokes, MP, they wanted our children to know 'the names of our kings and queens, the names of our warriors and battles, and the glorious deeds of our past'. They wanted to revive the bad old practice of teaching British history as a long series of at best apologetics for, at worst glorification of, British imperial conquest. They wanted to return to the days when David Thomson, author of *The*

Democratic Ideal in France and England (1940) and afterwards Master of Sidney Sussex College, Cambridge, could declare, in the eighth volume of the Pelican History of England (*England in the Nineteenth Century 1815-1914*, 1950), that 'British imperialism . . . was never racialist', while on the other hand 'other contemporary imperialisms *were* racialist' (emphasis added). There's 'patriotic' history for you!

And now we have the new national curriculum, in which black people and other ethnic minorities are marginalised, are placed outside the mainstream of the British nation and its history. The 'Making of the Nation' theme in the history section of the national curriculum does have something to say about settlers in Britain; but it concentrates on European settlers only. It gives the impression that by the end of the Norman invasion and settlement, in the eleventh century, the making of the British nation was complete. It leaves black people completely invisible, even though there were Africans here before the English came, even though there were at least 10,000 black people living here in Britain in the middle of the eighteenth century. British colonialism and its effects, in India, Africa, and the Caribbean, form no part of the national curriculum. But how on earth can the history of these islands be complete without the study of the conquest, colonisation, and exploitation of large areas of the world, which have resulted in the presence of people from those areas in Britain today?

On 23 August 1984, Sir Keith Joseph, then Secretary of State for Education, chose a conference of American historians to deliver himself of the observation that 'pride in one's country and its achievements' must be fostered in British schools. He added: 'The teacher should lead the pupil towards his or her own decisions about which aspects of national events, institutions, or culture, are most deserving of admiration'. Well, this isn't such a bad guideline, given one essential pre-condition: that the black contribution to British history, hitherto neglected in syllabuses, curricula, and textbooks, shall now at long last be included in them — provided, in short, that the black community in Britain is no longer denied a past. Let the pupils, black and white alike, who are making their 'own decisions' about what and what not to admire in British history, be told of the massive involuntary contribution made by black slaves in the Caribbean, and by the plunder of Bengal, to the growth of Britain's wealth and major industries and major cities in the eighteenth century. Let them be told how and on what basis English racism arose and what its role has been in the validation of colonialism. Let them be told the truth about the British Empire: that, above all, it was a mechanism for extracting profit out of the labour of the hundreds of millions of black people who were its unwilling and always rebellious subjects. Let them be told of the contributions made by black radicals to the building of the British labour movement and the winning of civil liberties in this country in the nineteenth century. Not least, let them be told of the thousands of black soldiers and sailors who, fighting under the Union Jack in two world wars, were wounded, crippled for life, or killed in battle — from Cardiff alone, in World War I, 1,000 black seafarers were killed at sea, and another 400, rescued after their ships were sunk, were taken back to the port to die of the effects of exposure.

These and many other aspects of British black history include achievements gained in the teeth of unremitting race prejudice, consistent racial discrimination, and murderous racist attacks. Such achievements are surely, to use Sir Keith Joseph's words, 'deserving of admiration'. So it is plainly the duty of enlightened and conscientious teachers to take Joseph at his word by throwing light on this hitherto shamefully obscure area of British history. For how can people make their own decisions about what is and what is not admirable in British history if they are not given the facts?

British black history must therefore now begin to take its rightful place within the school curriculum, as an essential part of the history of this country's poor and labouring majority, as well as a central part of British imperial history. Giving it that rightful place is a task which faces both black and white educators. It is a task they have to shoulder together.

Let's return to the questions I started with: 'What has black history got to do with white people?' and 'Why should we listen to a white person telling us about our own history?' I have tried to give a political answer to these political questions. Now, in conclusion, I want to try to give a personal answer.

Behind these questions — which, as I said, are really the same question put in different ways — is deep pain at grievous historical wrongs. I understand that pain, and I share it. Working on my book *Staying Power: The history of black people in Britain* (1984) was often painful for me. It was a disagreeable shock, for instance, to find that one slaver captain operating out of Liverpool in the year 1789 bore the same name as my own son. I've no idea whether Captain James Fryer, commander of the *Little Ben*, which carried 75 slaves, was in fact an ancestor of mine. What I do know about him is that he was a cog in a money-making machine devised, not simply by white Europeans, but by European *capitalism*.

Pain can be blinding. But we shouldn't let it blind us to historical truth. And if we see the slave trade, and the triangular trade of which it was one segment, as just a matter of wicked Europeans victimising Africans we shall never understand what was going on. European capitalism appropriated everything in Africa it could lay its hands on, from the continent's able-bodied labour, which it systematically drained away for its own purposes for the better part of 500 years, to the entire tangible cultural heritage of the Edo of Benin, now for the most part scattered in European museums and private collections.

But, as we shall see in the second lecture, African slaves were bought, not captured, by the slaver captains from Liverpool, London, and Bristol. For there to be buyers there must be sellers. And European capitalism, buying slaves on the African coast in exchange for British-made goods, had eager accomplices in the shape of African merchant capitalists and African monarchs, some of whom were so keen to get *their* greedy hands on what European capitalism had to offer that they kidnapped their own subjects for sale to foreign buyers.

So not all Africans were victims. And not all Europeans were villains or capitalists or willing cogs in the triangular trade. Some white Englishmen, like Thomas Clarkson and Granville Sharp, fought bravely and tenaciously against the slave trade, long before William Wilberforce climbed on the band-wagon at the last minute when he realised it would win him votes. Who can read Thomas Clarkson's account of how he trembled with fear as he rode into Bristol, to gather ammunition for the campaign against the slave trade, without a feeling of admiration for his courage? The man whom the Liverpool slave-merchants later did try to murder 'began to tremble . . . at the arduous task I had undertaken. . . . I anticipated much persecution in it . . . and I questioned whether I should even get out of it alive'. As we shall see in the final lecture, the London 'Mob' of the second half of the eighteenth century physically defended runaway slaves against the slave-hunting gangs hired by the West India sugar-planters. And this tradition of solidarity and joint resistance continued. The demand for the abolition of slavery and the emancipation of the slaves was central to the British working-class movement that emerged in the 1790s, which black people helped to organise and lead. The lives, struggles, and achievements of Olaudah Equiano, William Davidson, Robert Wedderburn, and William Cuffay, to all of whom I shall return in the sixth lecture, are part of British black history. But not only that: they are part of British working-class history too.

Are we really to accept the view that black people should not listen to a white person who knows something about this tradition and speaks in its name? Are we really to allow British black history to be ghettoised? Or shall it be taught by competent persons, regardless of skin colour and ethnic origin, to the many students who are thirsting for knowledge on these questions?

Surely, for those who value historical truth, there can be only one answer to this question.

2

How Britain became 'Great Britain':
the triangular trade

In 1939, on the eve of World War II, a distinguished English historian — he was many other things as well — was talking about what Britain had gained from having colonies in the West Indies. 'Our possession of the West Indies', he told his audience,

> . . . gave us the strength, the support, but especially the capital, the wealth, at a time when no other European nation possessed such a reserve, which enabled us to come through the great struggle of the Napoleonic Wars, the keen competition of the eighteenth and nineteenth centuries, and enabled us . . . to lay the foundation of that commercial and financial leadership which . . . enabled us to make our great position in the world.

These were the words of Winston Churchill, addressing a banquet of West Indies sugar planters in London in 1939. And possession of the West Indies and of India provided precisely those two 'special forced draughts' which, in Eric Hobsbawm's words (in his 1954 essay 'The Crisis of the 17th Century'), gave Britain's capitalists 'several precious decades of dizzy economic expansion from which they drew inestimable benefits'. This process of accumulating the wealth from which Britain's industrial revolution was funded is known to students of Marx's *Capital* as 'primitive accumulation' (though I fancy a better English rendering would be 'primary accumulation'). 'Capital', wrote Marx, 'comes [into the world] dripping from head to foot, from every pore, with blood and dirt.' And, in the same chapter, entitled 'Genesis of the Industrial

Capitalist', he wrote of 'the turning of Africa into a warren for the commercial hunting of black-skins' and added: 'Liverpool waxed fat on the slave-trade. This was its method of primitive accumulation. . . The veiled slavery of the wage-workers in Europe needed, for its pedestal, slavery pure and simple in the new world.'

Well, we now know that it wasn't only Liverpool that waxed fat on the slave trade: so did Bristol, and so did London, to an extent that has only recently been discovered by the Canadian economic historian James A. Rawley. And we now know that it wasn't only the slave trade that yielded a massive transfusion of wealth, but the entire triangular trade of which the slave trade was the fulcrum. Let us look at the whole process more closely.

The British West Indies were a single-crop economy, and that crop was sugar, the 'white gold' of the New World. Barbados began exporting sugar in 1646; by 1660 St Kitts was exporting more sugar than indigo; Jamaica started planting sugar in 1664. Tobacco, cotton, ginger, cocoa, and coffee were also grown but were of comparatively minor importance. Sugar was king, and its rule was never seriously challenged.

In order to grow sugar, British planters in the Caribbean needed two things above all.

In the first place, they needed virtually unlimited long-term credit to sustain them during the years it took to grow a first crop and to 'season' (i.e. acclimatise) the labour. Such credit was their life-blood, and it was provided by commission agents, or 'factors', in the City of London. These commission agents, mostly rich merchants, put up the money for the purchase of plantations and slaves, and made their fortunes on the interest they charged. They became in effect the planters' bankers. These were the fat spiders at the centre of the whole web: men like Henry Lascelles, MP, who sucked so much wealth from the commission system, from the import of sugar, and from outright fraud, that his successors became earls of Harewood and married into the royal family. This credit system primed the pump, and did so very profitably indeed.

In the second place, the planters needed cheap labour to plant and tend the crops, cut the canes, and process the sugar. After a brief unsuccessful experiment with indentured English convicts, they found the labour they needed in Africa. To pay for slaves, Britain's manufacturing industries sent their products to the African coast. They sent textiles made in Lancashire, guns and wrought-iron goods made in Birmingham, brass goods made in Bristol, copper goods made in Swansea, Flint, and Lancashire, pewter made in Liverpool, and cutlery made in Sheffield. With these products went gunpowder, bullets, tallow, tobacco-pipes, glass beads, toys, malt spirits, and beer from the Whitbread and Truman breweries. The yearly value of British manufactured goods exported to Africa soared from £83,000 in 1710 to £401,000 in 1787. These goods were bartered for human beings on what was then known as the Guinea coast, which we now call the West African coast.

'Guinea' was soon the popular name for the new gold coin struck in 1663 by a slave-trading company called the Royal Adventurers into Africa, whose stockholders, according to A. P. Thornton's *West-India Policy under the Restoration* (1956), 'included every major figure in the Court and in the Administration, as well as every moneyed man in London and Bristol'. For 200 years real English wealth, the sort of wealth that went with high rank and social prestige, would be measured, not in pounds, but in guineas, which is to say 'Africans'. Some of the earliest guinea coins bore on the obverse, below the bust of King Charles II in profile, a tiny African elephant. In Liverpool, soon to become Europe's major slaving port, the City fathers were less squeamish: when they built a new town hall in the middle of the eighteenth century they decorated it with the heads, carved in stone, of African elephants and African slaves.

But it wasn't only the three big slaving ports — London, Bristol, and Liverpool — that prospered. The industries producing the goods with which the slaves were bought, and the cities associated with those industries, prospered too. The 'opulence' of Manchester, as well as that of Liverpool, was admitted in 1841 to be 'as really owing to the toil and suffering of the negro, as if his hands had excavated their docks and fabricated their steam-engines'. The slave trade, says one economic historian, was one of the 'powerful factors influencing the early success' of the Birmingham gun trade. The slave trade gave the Swansea copper industry such a 'special forced draught' that by the middle of the nineteenth century it was supplying over half the copper needs of the entire world. Copper production had been greatly boosted by the practice of copper-sheathing ships' bottoms, an innovation first adopted by Britain's slaving fleet. Other industries, too, benefited directly from the slave trade: shipbuilding, for instance, and its ancillary industries sailmaking and ropemaking. In 1788 it was estimated that 'the Artificers and Mechanics' employed in Liverpool received £100,000 a year for the labour and materials used in equipping slave-ships.

British traders bought slaves in Africa not only for resale to British planters in the Caribbean, and in the North American colonies, but also for sale to Spanish colonists in the New World. Spain was the only colonising power that lacked any kind of base on the West African coast. So the Spaniards had to turn to middlemen for their supply of slaves. And the English were happy to oblige. The first licence to Spaniards to buy slaves in the 'Caribbees' and Jamaica was granted as early as 1663, and the traffic continued, on and off, for the next 50 years. Then, in 1713, under the treaty of Utrecht, Britain acquired the *assiento*, an official contract to supply 4,800 Africans a year to Spanish colonies in south and central America, the Spanish West Indies, Mexico, and Florida. Until 1791, a quarter of the Atlantic slave trade was in British hands, and from 1791 to 1806 Britain's share was over half.

The most recent estimate of the profits made by British slave-merchants on the sale of the 2.5 million Africans they are thought to have handled between 1630 and 1807 puts it at about £12 million. And these 'fabulous' profits, as Walter Rodney calls them, were of course merely a fraction of the wealth generated by the triangular trade as a whole, as we shall see.

There were profits also, of course, for the African slave-merchants and rulers who sold Africans to the European slaver captains. In the short term these profits helped the development of local merchant capitalism. The long-term effects of this trade included the irreversible distortion of the African economy; the creation of client kingdoms, paving the way for colonialism; and the draining from the continent of a vast amount of able-bodied labour.

The Africans bought by the British slave captains on the West African coast were mostly very young: healthy, able-bodied young men and women between the ages of 15 and 25. They were branded like cattle, then carried across the Atlantic, the men chained in the hold for 20 hours out of the 24. For various reasons the death-rate of those transported on British slavers fell over the years. Yes, it fell — from an average of one in four in the 1680s to one in twelve a hundred years later. But the death-rate of the children was uniformly high. It was taken for granted that, of those who survived the 'middle passage', one in three would die, of dysentery or suicide (a form of resistance) in their first three years in the New World. Those first three years were the 'seasoning' period. Those who survived them were set to work under the whip to produce 'white gold' for their white masters. Flogging — in Jamaica, with a ten-foot cart-whip — was routine punishment for almost every offence, and was inflicted on girls, women, boys, and men alike. The slaves were grossly underfed, as both an economy and an attempt, rarely successful, to break their spirit.

From the forced labour of those millions of Africans in the sugar plantations, millions of pounds were made, over a period not far short of 200 years. Britain's sugar imports from the Caribbean trebled between 1700 and 1764. For Britain, wrote the American historian Frank Wesley Pitman, this brought 'perhaps . . . the greatest increment of wealth in modern times'. Michael Craton has calculated that 'over the entire period of slavery the West Indian plantations alone may have brought the planters an aggregate profit of over £150,000,000 at a rate that averaged £1,000,000 a year throughout the eighteenth century'. Taking the triangular trade as a whole, he adds that 'between 1640 and 1838 private English individuals and concerns interested in slavery may have generated as much as £450 millions in profits: two thirds of it in the eighteenth century and half in the half century after 1750'.

What happened to the profits?

Some were squandered on luxurious living by the absentee planters who came back to Britain with their retinues of black household slaves.

Some of the profits were used to finance the pro-slavery West India lobby, probably the first organised parliamentary lobby in history. This was the powerful lever by which the 'West Indians' exercised an influence on British politics, on the law-making process, on the administration of justice and, through the press, on public opinion. The lobby's strength, as *The Cambridge History of the British Empire* tells us, became 'a dominant factor in the control of colonial policy'.

Some of the profits were reinvested in the colony trade — were used, that is, to buy the manufactured goods needed to run the plantations. Here was a further boost for British industry: by 1784 no less than half of Britain's exports were going to the colonies (including the newly independent United States).

Lastly, and above all, some of the profits were invested directly in British industry. The coal and iron industries of south Wales depended directly on the triangular trade for their initial funding. In 1765 Anthony Bacon MP was granted a contract to furnish 'seasoned, able and working negroes' to the islands of Grenada, the Grenadines, Tobago, St Vincent, and Dominica, and the British government paid him almost £67,000 for these slaves. The money went straight into industrial development around Merthyr Tydfil, then a mere hamlet. Bacon took a 99-year lease on 4,000 acres of virgin mineral land, developed coalmines and iron-foundries that came to be known as 'Bacon's mineral kingdom', and made his fortune in the process. The north Wales slate industry, producing roofing slates for factory workers' dwellings, was financed by profits from the triangular trade. The south Yorkshire iron industry; the Liverpool and Manchester Railway; the Great Western Railway; the original steam engine of James Watt: all were financed in part with profits accumulated from the triangular trade. The early history of the British banking system, from the first country banks and Barclays right up to the Bank of England, is closely connected with the triangular trade, as is the early history of British insurance.

At the time, they made no bones about it. The slave trade and the sugar trade were seen as inseparably connected, and as together forming the foundation of English greatness. The Royal African Company's chief agent on the West African coast wrote in 1690 that 'the Kingdoms Pleasure, Glory, and Grandure' were more advanced by the sugar produced by black slaves 'than by any other Commodity we deal in or produce, Wooll not excepted'. John Oldmixon wrote of Barbados in 1708: 'When we examine the Riches that have been rais'd by the Produce of this little Spot of Ground, we shall find that it has been as good as a Mine of Silver or Gold to the Crown of *England*.' The Royal African Company's surgeon wrote in 1725 that the slave trade was

> a glorious and advantageous Trade . . . the Hinge on which all the Trade of this Globe moves . . . for . . . put a Stop to the Slave Trade, and all the others cease of Course . . . who sweetens the Ladies Tea, and the generous Bowl [i.e. rum punch]; and who reaps the Profit of all? Therefore, let every true *Briton* unanimously join to concert Measures, how to center this advantageous Trade in *England*.

It should be borne in mind that sugar production, in Richard Sheridan's words, 'was more demanding of hard physical labour and more destructive to life and limb than that of most other tropical and semi-tropical staples'. For instance, the labour force had to undertake the entire task of preparing the land for planting; the land wasn't ploughed, but holed laboriously with the hoe, a task that imposed a heavy physical strain. Sheridan's observation is true also of the industrial sector of sugar production. In 1802 Lady Nugent, wife of Jamaica's lieutenant-governor, wrote in her journal after a visit to a sugar mill:

> I asked the overseer how often his people were relieved. He said every twelve hours; but how dreadful to think of their standing twelve hours over a boiling cauldron . . .; and he owned to me that sometimes they did fall asleep, and got their poor fingers into the mill; and he shewed me a hatchet, that was always ready to sever the whole limb, as the only means of saving the poor sufferer's life!

To the planters, as D. A. G. Waddell puts it in his book *The West Indies & the Guianas* (1967), slaves were essentially 'a form of capital equipment', more easily and more cheaply replaceable than machinery. So it was more cost-effective to chop off a finger, hand, or arm than to stop the machinery for as long as it took to set a trapped sugar-boiler free.

Nor was it only in Cuba, under Spanish masters, that black slaves were literally worked to death. That was their fate also in Demerara, afterwards part of British Guiana, on a plantation owned by the Gladstone family — a plantation that rejoiced in the name 'Success'. Throughout the West Indies slave mortality, especially infant mortality, was consistently high. In Barbados, for example, in the middle of the eighteenth century, 5,000 slaves were dying each year out of a total black population of 80,000.

The emerging industrial working class in Britain was exploited by the same capitalist class that exploited black slaves in the British West Indies, and was regarded by it in much the same light. When we ask, for instance, who it was that produced those textiles exported to Africa for the purchase of slaves, we find that a great many of the workers in the Lancashire textile mills — workers not yet organised in trades unions and, before the Factory Acts, ruthlessly exploited — that a great many of them were not adults, but children. And many of those children were nothing but little serfs: the children of the urban poor, whose destitute parents had been admitted to the parish workhouses. The children were taken from them and compulsorily bound apprentice to the cotton-manufacturers. When these overworked children fell asleep under the machines they were beaten back to work by overseers armed with billy-rollers or straps. The cotton mills they worked in were hotbeds of typhus. J. L. and Barbara Hammond, in a remarkable passage in their forgotten book *The Rise of Modern Industry* (1925), traced the connexion between the child-serf system and the slave system that it directly served:

An age that thought of the African negro, not as a person with a human life, but as so much labour power to be used in the service of a master or a system, came naturally to think of the poor at home in the same way. . . .

The children of the poor were regarded as workers long before the Industrial Revolution. Locke [the great English empiricist philosopher] suggested that they should begin work at three. . . . In the workhouses of large towns there was a quantity of child labour available for employment, that was even more powerless . . . in the hands of a master than the stolen negro. . . . The new industry which was to give the English people such immense power in the world borrowed at its origin from the methods of the American [i.e. Caribbean] settlements.

When a London parish gave relief it generally claimed the right of disposing of all the children of the person receiving relief, and thus these London workhouses could be made to serve the purpose of the Lancashire cotton mills as the Guinea coast served that of the West India plantations. The analogy became painfully complete. In the *Assiento* the negroes are described as 'pieces', and the description would not be less suitable to the children taken for the mills.

Sent to the north by wagon-loads at a time, the children were 'as much lost for ever to their parents as if they were shipped off to the West Indies'. And one MP, speaking in the Commons in 1811, used arguments in favour of this child serf system identical in substance — as we shall see in the fourth lecture — with those used by the apologists for black slavery, who claimed that enslavement was good for Africans since it humanised and civilised them:

Although in the higher ranks of society it was true that to cultivate the affections of children for their family was the source of every virtue, yet, that it was not so among the lower orders, and that it was a benefit to the children to take them away from their miserable and depraved parents.

3

How Britain became 'Great Britain: the plunder and de-industrialisation of India

We saw last time that British possession of the West Indies and of India provided those two 'special forced draughts' which got the industrial revolution in Britain off the ground by giving British capitalism, in the words of Eric Hobsbawm, 'several precious decades of dizzy economic expansion from which they drew inestimable benefits'. In the previous lecture we examined the first of those two 'special forced draughts'; now we are going to look at the second.

Before they were able to plunder India directly, British merchant capitalists were forced to use some of the profits from elsewhere in the colonial system to pay for the goods they bought from the Indians. They coveted India's wealth, but at that stage they had to offer wealth in return. Once the British had secured the *assiento* in 1713, they could offer silver bullion paid by Spain for those 4,800 African slaves the British were now under contract to supply each year. The slave trade and privateering thus gave them the necessary leverage in India. A European power with a surplus of silver had the advantage over all competitors.

The battle of Plassey in 1757, at which British troops defeated the ruler of Bengal, was the decisive turning-point, not only for British domination of India, but also for British extraction of wealth from India. The adventurer Robert Clive, who had put a British puppet on the throne of Bengal, told the British prime minister in 1759 that there would be 'little or no difficulty in obtaining the absolute possession of these rich kingdoms'. The battle of Plassey put an end once and for all to the need to send precious silver to India. Very soon there was widespread rejoicing that the British army's 'glorious successes' had

> brought near three millions of money to the nation; for . . . almost the whole of the immense sums received . . . finally centers in England. So great a proportion of it fell into the company's hands . . . that they have been enabled to carry on the whole trade of India (China excepted) for three years together, without sending out one ounce of bullion.

For the East India Company this was a dream come true. Now they could get their hands on India's wealth without having to send wealth in return. The first step was the assumption of the *dewani*, the right to collect the revenue in Bengal, Behar, and Orissa. Traditionally in India there had been an intimate relation between harvest and taxation. Before British rule there was no private property in land. The self-governing village community handed over each year to the ruler or his nominee the 'King's share' of the year's produce. The East India Company considered this practice barbarous and put a stop to it. Under British rule a new revenue system was introduced, superseding the traditional right of the village community over land and creating two new forms of property in land: in some parts of the country, landlordism; in others, individual peasant proprietorship. It was assumed that the State was the supreme landlord, and there was introduced a system of fixed tax payments, assessed on land. Under the new system the cultivator had to pay a fixed sum to the government every year whether or not his crop had been successful. In years when the harvest was bad, the cultivators could pay their taxes only by recourse to money-lenders, whom the British authorities regarded as the mainstay for the payment of revenue, and who frequently charged interest of 200 per cent or more. 'We introduced at one bound', a British writer later admitted, 'new methods of assessing and cultivating the land revenue, which have converted a once flourishing population into a huge horde of paupers.' Since peasants, in order to raise the cash demanded of them, were forced to sell their produce for whatever it would fetch, 'the first effect of British rule in an Indian province . . . was . . . to reduce the incomes of the agricultural classes by 50 per cent'. The British conquest undermined the agrarian economy and the self-governing village.

The assumption of the *dewani* gave the East India Company not only the entire revenue of the eastern provinces but also enormous political and economic power. This power was soon used to get rid of French, Dutch, and Danish 'factories'; to prevent Indian and other merchants from trading in grain, salt, betel nuts, and tobacco; and to discourage handicrafts. In 1769 the Company prohibited the home work of the silk weavers and compelled them to work in its factories. The Company's servants, who lined their pockets by private trading, bribery, and extortion, arbitrarily decided how much cloth each weaver should deliver and how much he should receive for it. Weavers who disobeyed were seized, imprisoned, fined, or flogged. Weavers unable to meet the obligations the Company imposed on them had their possessions confiscated and sold on the spot. Bengal's ruler complained that the Company's agents were taking away people's goods by force for a quarter of their value and compelling people to buy from them at five times the value of the goods bought, on pain of a flogging or imprisonmment. By the 1770s Bengal, in the words of a contemporary writer, had become 'one continued scene of oppression'.

Systematic plunder led to a famine in which 10 millon people perished. Stanley Wolpert tells us in his *New History of India* (second edition, 1982) that 'Bengal was left naked, stripped of its surplus wealth and grain. In the wake of British spoliation, famine struck and in 1770 alone took the lives of an estimated one-third of Bengal's peasantry.' This was the first of that long series of terrible famines in which, throughout the years of British rule, and right up to the Bengal famine of 1943, millions of Indians starved to death. A Commons Select Committee reported in 1783 that 'the Natives of all Ranks and Orders' had been reduced to a 'State of Depression and Misery'. Four years later a former army officer, William Fullarton, wrote as follows:

In former times the Bengal countries were the granary of nations, and the repository of commerce, wealth and manufacture in the East. . . . But such has been the restless energy of our misgovernment, that within the short space of twenty years many parts of those countries have been reduced to the appearance of a desert. The fields are no longer cultivated, — extensive tracts are already overgrown with thickets, — the husband-man is plundered, — the manufacturer [i.e. handicraftsman] oppressed, — famine has been repeatedly endured, — and depopulation has ensued.

As India became poor and hungry, Britain became richer than ever before. Colossal fortunes were made. Clive, penniless when he first landed in India, sent back to Britain nearly a third of the revenue he collected, and went back home with a personal fortune estimated at £250,000. When his activities were investigated by an envious House of Commons, Clive uttered those immortal words: 'By God, Mr

Chairman, at this moment I stand amazed at my own moderation.' A young writer or ensign could go out to India and, within three years, come back home with a fortune big enough for him to set himself up as a country gentleman. It was in this period that the Hindi word 'loot' entered the English language (it was first recorded in print in 1839). And it is estimated that, between the battle of Plassey in 1757 and the battle of Waterloo in 1815, i.e. in 58 years, Britain's loot from India was worth somewhere between £500 million and £1,000 million.

Who can doubt that this loot from India furnished the second of those 'special forced draughts' which were needed to ignite Britain's industrial revolution. Was it mere coincidence that, close on the heels of the battle of Plassey in 1757, came the harnessing in rapid succession of a critical series of inventions and technological advances? Hargreaves's spinning jenny (1764), Arkwright's water-frame (1769), and Crompton's mule (1779) broke with the old hand techniques. In 1785 came the next logical step: the adaptation of Watt's steam-engine to drive them. The increase in productivity was explosive. Between 1767 and 1787 the output of cotton goods went up more than fivefold.

We must bear in mind that when European merchant adventurers first reached India they did not find an industrial or technical backwater. On the contrary, 'the industrial development of the country was at any rate not inferior to that of the more advanced European nations': so said the official *Report of the Indian Industrial Commission*, published in 1919. India was not only a great agricultural country but also a great manufacturing country. It had a prosperous textile industry, whose cotton, silk, and woollen products were marketed in Europe as well as elsewhere in Asia. It had remarkable, and remarkably ancient, skills in iron-working. It had its own shipbuilding industry: Calcutta, Daman, Surat, Bombay, and Pegu were important shipbuilding centres. In 1802 skilled Indian workers were building British warships at the Bombay shipyard of Bomenjee and Manseckjee, and according to a historian of Indian shipping it was generally acknowledged that 'the teak-wood vessels of Bombay were greatly superior to the oaken walls of Old England'. Benares was famous all over India for its brass, copper, and bell-metal wares. Other important industries included the enamelled jewelry and stone-carving of the Rajputana towns, as well as filigree work in gold and silver, ivory, glass, tannery, perfumery, and paper-making.

All this was altered under British rule. The long-term consequence of that rule was the de-industrialisation of India — its forcible transformation from a country of combined agriculture and manufacture into an agricultural colony of British capitalism, exporting raw cotton, wool, jute, oilseeds, dyes, and hides to Britain. The British annihilated the Indian textile industry 'with the fury of a forest fire'; a dangerous competitor existed, and it had to be destroyed. The shipbuilding industry aroused the jealousy of British firms, 'and its progress and development were restricted by legislation'. India's metalwork, glass, and paper industries were likewise throttled, the paper industry being deprived of its greatest patron when an order of Sir Charles Wood, secretary of state for India, 1859-66, obliged the British government in India to use only British-made paper.

The vacuum created by the contrived ruin of the Indian handicraft industries, a process virtually completed by 1880, was filled with British manufactured goods. Britain's industrial revolution, with its explosive increase in productivity, made it essential for British capitalists to find new markets. So, in India, the previous monopoly had to give way to a free market. From an exporter of textiles, India had to become an importer of textiles. British goods had to have virtually free entry, while the entry into Britain of goods manufactured in India, especially silks and cottons, had to be blocked by prohibitive tariffs. And direct trade between India and the rest of the world had to be curtailed. By 1840 British silk and cotton goods imported into India paid a duty of only three-and-a-half per cent, woollen goods a mere two per cent. Equivalent Indian exports to Britain paid import duties of 20, 10, and 30 per cent respectively.

> Had not such prohibitory duties and decrees existed [wrote Horace Hayman Wilson in 1845, in his *The History of British India from 1805 to 1835* (1845)] the mills of Paisley and of Manchester would have been stopped. . . . They were created by the sacrifice of the Indian manufacture. . . . The foreign manufacturer employed the arm of political injustice to keep down and ultimately strangle a competitor with whom he could not have contended on equal terms.

So there was prosperity for the British cotton industry and ruin for millions of Indian craftsmen and artisans. India's rich manufacturing towns were blighted: towns like Decca, once known as 'the Manchester of India', and Murshidabad, Bengal's old capital, said in 1757 to be as extensive, populous, and rich as London. Millions of spinners and weavers were forced to seek a precarious living in the countryside, as were many tanners, smelters, and smiths.

The development of Indian cotton mills in the 1870s, coupled with a trade slump in Britain, led Lancashire textile manufacturers to press for total repeal of Indian cotton duties, which had given some small protection to the Indian cotton industry as well as 'retaining labour in the industrial sector which could more usefully be employed in growing cotton for export to Lancashire'. The Lancashire capitalists had their way. In 1879 Viceroy Lytton 'overruled his entire council to accommodate Lancashire's lobby by removing all import duties on British-made cotton, despite India's desperate need for more revenue in a year of widespread famine'. In the last twenty years of the nineteenth century India's own production of cloth met less than 10 per cent of home demand, while Lancashire products accounted for between one-half and two-thirds of India's annual imports.

Britain, whose queen had been proclaimed 'Empress of India' in 1876, had made India subservient to British industry and its needs and was continuing to suck vast wealth out of the sub-continent. Generations of Indian economists and nationalist politicians, supported by a small number of British opponents of colonialism, complained of this drain of wealth, analysed its mechanisms in copious detail, proved their case with massive evidence from official sources, and showed how this economic exploitation was the root cause of the Indian people's poverty and hunger. Under British imperial rule the ordinary people of India grew steadily poorer. The economic historian Romesh Dutt, writing in 1906, called Indian poverty 'unparalleled'. Half of India's annual net revenues of £44 million, he calculated, flowed out of India. The number of famines soared from seven in the first half of the nineteenth century to 24 in the second half. According to official figures, 28,825,000 Indians starved to death between 1854 and 1901. The terrible famine of 1899-1900, which affected 475,000 square miles with a population of almost 60 million, was attributed to a process of bleeding the peasants, who were forced into the clutches of money-lenders whom the British authorities regarded as their mainstay for the payment of revenue. The Bengal famine of 1943, which claimed 1.5 million victims, was accentuated by the authorities' carelessness and utter lack of foresight, and the Famine Inquiry Commission severely criticised the 'administrative breakdown'.

Rich though its soil was, India's people were hungry, and miserably poor. This grinding poverty 'struck all visitors . . . like a blow in the face'. That was how it struck the delegation which visited India on behalf of the India League in 1932. The delegation — one of whose members, Ellen Wilkinson, was to be education minister in the 1945 Labour government — spent 83 days in India, meeting Indians of every class and shade of opinion. In their report, *Condition of India* (1934), they said they had been

> appalled at the poverty of the Indian village. It is the home of stark want. . . . From province to province conditions vary, but the results of uneconomic agriculture, peasant indebtedness, excessive taxation and rack-renting, absence of social services and the general discontent impressed us everywhere. . . . In the villages we saw, there were no health or sanitary services, there were no roads, no drainage or lighting, and no proper water supply beyond the village well. . . .
>
> Men, women and children work in the fields, farms and cowsheds. . . . All alike work on meagre food and comfort and toil long hours for inadequate returns.

In short, throughout the British occupation, millions of Indians could never get enough food, and at least two-thirds of the people connected, directly or indirectly, with agriculture lived 'in a state of squalor'. In 1946, on the eve of the British withdrawal, Jawaharlal Nehru wrote that those parts of India which had been longest under British rule were the poorest: 'Bengal, once so rich and flourishing, after 187 years of British rule . . . is . . . a miserable mass of poverty-stricken, starving, and dying people.' In India, as everywhere else in the British Empire, British capitalists got rich by robbing black people.

For the great majority of black people who lived in it, the British Empire meant chronic poverty, chronic hunger, rampant disease, atrocious housing, virtually 100 per cent illiteracy, and, when they protested, brutal tyranny and repression. For the British capitalist class it meant massive wealth. To establish, maintain, and justify their rule over, and their exploitation of, 370 million black people, Britain's rulers needed an ideology which told them — and also told the British working class and the children in Britain's schools — that their imperial rule was in the best interests of their colonial subjects. This imperialist ideology was racism, whose origins and development and various forms will be examined in the next lecture.

4

The history of English racism

In the last two lectures we've been looking at the economic aspects of British black history: the savage exploitation of black labour, and the ruthless plunder of territories inhabited by black people, within the British Empire. Now I want to discuss the ways in which the robbery and oppression of black people were justified by racist ideology. I will also say something about the ways in which racism has manifested itself here in Britain since the post-war black settlement began with the arrival of the *Empire Windrush* at Tilbury on 22 June 1948.

From the historical point of view, racism presents itself at first as a mere scientific error. The very concept of 'race' is a hangover from the prehistory of the biological sciences. Geneticists and anthropologists, when they are discussing the variations in human physical characteristics, no longer use this outmoded concept. They have discarded it. They no longer divide human beings into 'races' on the trivial basis of skin pigmentation or any other distinction of form. They now recognise that the so-called 'races' merely represent temporary mixtures of genetic materials that are common to all humankind. They now recognise that there is no scientific basis for dividing people into fixed biological groups called 'races' or for saying that each of these groups possesses inherent, fixed cultural attributes. They now recognise that physical differences do not reflect underlying and significant mental differences; and that it is a delusion to suppose that they do.

But these delusions are not merely scientific errors. For some 300 years racism has had a precise social function. It has functioned as an ideology: a system of false ideas justifying the exploitation and domination of people with a visible degree of melanin in their skin by people whose melanocytes are not so active. The concept of 'race', expunged from the vocabulary of scientists, persists in everyday speech as a *political* category: a category that helps to determine who has power over whom. The ascription of individuals to racial groups is a political act. Racial labels are political weapons by means of which a dominant group can retain a subject group in subjection.

Racist ideology sprang from slavery. It arose as a justification of the enslavement of black people in the New World. At the very heart of the new capitalist system that was clawing its way to world supremacy there were three tragic anomalies:

1. The rising capitalist class depended for its very existence on free labour — yet it made extensive use of slave labour as its springboard.

2. The rising capitalist class harnessed to production a whole series of technological advances — yet it depended extensively on the most backward and inefficient method of production.

3. The rising capitalist class proudly inscribed freedom of the individual on its banner; yet it not only, in the words of Elisabeth Fox-Genovese and Eugene D. Genovese, 'conquered, absorbed, and reinforced servile labor systems throughout the world' but also 'created new ones, including systems of chattel slavery, on an unprecedented social scale and at an unprecedented level of violence'. This class therefore 'required a violent racism not merely as an ideological rationale but as a psychological imperative'.

This last anomaly, this contradiction between freedom of the individual and freedom of property, found dramatic expression in a famous courtroom scene at the London Mansion House in the year 1767. A young black man called Jonathan Strong had been kidnapped and thrown in jail on behalf of a Jamaica planter. He appealed for help to the anti-slavery campaigner Granville Sharp and was brought before the lord mayor, who ruled that Strong was not guilty of any offence and was therefore free to go. Whereupon the captain of the ship which was to have transported Strong to Jamaica grasped his arm, in open court, and declared that he would secure him as the planter's property. Sharp warned the captain that, if he presumed to take Strong, he would find himself charged with assault. Then the captain, in Sharp's words, 'withdrew his hand, and all parties retired from the presence of the Lord Mayor, and Jonathan Strong departed also, in the sight of all, in full liberty, nobody daring afterwards to touch him'.

Here, in dramatic collision, are the two basic principles of the new, rising, capitalist world order: property rights; and freedom of the individual. Five years later, Lord Chief Justice Mansfield would partially restrict the former and partially uphold the latter — not, as the official myth has always claimed and as every schoolboy knows, by setting black slaves in Britain free — but by ruling that one slave, called James Somerset, might not lawfully be taken out of England against his will. This was a limited resolution, at the legal level, of that clash between two cardinal principles of the capitalist world outlook which was acted out at the Mansion House in 1767.

But British sugar planters in the Caribbean, and their mouthpieces in Britain, were resolving the contradiction at the ideological level in a very different way. At the Mansion House the captain referred to Strong as a piece of property. No, retorted Sharp, Strong was a human being and therefore free. If the planter had been there and had spoken his mind he would have said something to this effect: 'This is no human being but a kind of ape or sub-man for which I have undertaken to pay £30 as soon as it is securely on board ship.' That this is no exaggeration is shown by the words of another Jamaica planter, John Gardner Kemeys, who wrote in a pro-slavery pamphlet published in 1783:

Many of the negroes imported from Africa partake of the brute creation [i.e. are like animals]; not long since a cargo of them arrived in Jamaica, whose hands had little or no ball to the thumbs, whose nails were more of the claw kind than otherwise, and their want of intellectual faculties was very apparent. Every planter knows that there are negroes, who . . . cannot be humanised as others are, that they will remain, with respect to their understanding, but a few degrees removed from the ourang-outang [i.e. the chimpanzee and gorilla]; and from which many negroes may be supposed, without any very improbable conjecture[,] to be the offspring. . . . The Colonists of the West-Indies are instrumental in humanising the descendants of the offspring of even brutes . . . to the honour of the human species, and to the glory of the divine being. . . .

If the controul we maintain over them is proved to be for their good, and to the welfare of society; that it is, probably, taming of brutes . . . theirs [sic] and our rights will appear in very different points of view.

Just as it was a benefit to the children of the poor to take them away from their miserable and depraved parents (cf. p. 18 above), so it was a benefit to Africans to make plantation slaves of them, for they were thereby tamed and humanised.

Here is something more than mere cant; here is an ideology, a system of false ideas serving class interests. Here, in fact, is the earliest stage of racism: plantocracy racism. This ideology can be traced in the planters' oral tradition by the middle of the seventeenth century. It is reported, and convincingly analysed as a class ideology, in *The Negro's & Indians Advocate* (1680) by the Anglican minister Morgan Godwyn.

There was a widespread but false belief that a slave who was baptised was thereby set free. This belief had no doubt been strengthened by court judgments of 1677 and 1694 which suggested that since black people were 'infidels' or 'heathens' they might be treated as property. Ministers of religion who, like Godwyn, visited the Caribbean and told the planters they ought to have their slaves baptised were seen as threatening the planters' property rights. They were told that baptism would be pointless, since slaves were not human beings but animals without souls to save.

Racism first emerged in Britain itself in the eighteenth century. The pivotal figure in its development was the philosopher John Locke, who played a large part in the creation of the Board of Trade, the architect of the old colonial system. As a senior administrator of slave-owning colonies in the New World, Locke helped to draft instructions to the governor of Virginia in which black slavery was regarded as justifiable. Locke's contribution to emerging racism was his provision of a model which allows skin colour to be counted as an essential property of human beings. Racism was openly expressed in the writings of the philosopher David Hume, who also served for a time as a senior administrator of colonial affairs. In Hume's opinion, black people were 'naturally inferior' to whites, who held a monopoly of civilisation, art, science, and talent. Thus the essential conceptual building blocks used at first in the construction of racist ideology were provided by two of the greatest and most respected British philosophers. The classic expression of plantocracy racism was the *History of Jamaica* (1774) by Edward Long, a former judge and planter on that island. Long adduced 'scientific' evidence for black inferiority, and his *History* was in fact the key text in the turn to the pseudo-scientific racism that served, in the nineteenth and twentieth centuries, as a justification of colonialism.

By 1914 the British Empire covered 12.7 million square miles, of which the United Kingdom accounted for less than one-hundredth. It had a population of 431 million, of which the white self-governing population of the UK and the 'Dominions' totalled 60 million, or less than one-seventh. To establish, maintain, and justify their rule over, and exploitation of, 370 million black people, Britain's rulers needed a racism more subtle and diversified — but no less aggressive — than the plantocratic variety. Nineteenth-century racism took many forms, and we haven't time to do more than list them and briefly summarise what they taught.

As *phrenology*, racism told the British that they were ruling over peoples who, unlike themselves, lacked force of character. This pseudo-science deduced people's characters from the shape of their skulls. Its practitioners held that the skulls of Africans clearly demonstrated their inferiority to Europeans, and that the 'inferior' races would in time become extinct. As *teleology*, racism told the British that black people had been put on earth expressly to work for white people, especially in the tropics, where the sun was too hot for white people to do any work. This view, held by Thomas Carlyle and Anthony Trollope, was summed up thus in 1865, in the *Spectator*: 'The negroes are made on purpose to serve the whites, just as the black ants are made on purpose to serve the red.' As *evolutionism*, racism told the British that black people were to be hated, feared, fought and, ultimately, exterminated. This was the view of the Scottish anatomist Dr Robert Knox, as expressed in his book *The Races of Men* (1850); and of the traveller William Hepworth Dixon, as expressed in his book *White Conquest* (1876). As *anthropology*, racism told the British that black people were closer to apes than to Europeans; that they were intellectually inferior to Europeans; that they needed to be humanised, civilised, and governed with a very firm hand indeed; and that these tasks could be performed only by white people. The chief nineteenth-century exponent of this variety of racism was James Hunt, founder of the Anthropological Society of London and staunch defender of Governor Eyre of Jamaica in his ferocious suppression of the Jamaican rebellion of 1865. As *social darwinism*, racism told the British that black people were intellectually inferior to white people and doomed to extinction. This view was propagated by Benjamin Kidd in his book *Social Evolution* (1894); by Sir Francis Galton, founder of the 'science' of eugenics; and by Galton's pupil Karl Pearson, for whom exterminated inferior races were stepping-stones for the physically and mentally fitter race. *Anglo-Saxonism* was a form of racism that originally arose to justify the British conquest and occupation of Ireland, whose people it saw as 'unstable, childish, violent, lazy, feckless, feminine, and primitive', a view that had first crystallised in the twelfth century. This form of racism told the British that God had fitted precisely them to rule over others; that the British constitutional and legal systems were the freest, fairest, and most efficient in the world; and that lesser, 'degenerate' races were better dead. Such views formed part of the ideological baggage of Thomas Carlyle, who thought the English had the grand task of conquering half the planet or more; of Thomas Arnold, headmaster of Rugby public school; of Sir Edward Bulwer-Lytton, who served as colonial secretary in 1858-59 (and whose son served as viceroy of India, 1876-80); of Charles Dilke, author of *Greater Britain* (1868); of the novelist Charles Kingsley; and of the empire-builder Cecil Rhodes. In its cosmetic version, as *trusteeship*, racism told the British that they had a duty to promote the moral and educational progress of the child-like 'natives' over whom they ruled. Since black people were 'inferior', the British who ruled them owed them a special obligation, not unlike the obligation that decent Englishmen owed to women, children, and animals. This was the view of such colonial administrators as Sir Charles Eliot, as expressed in his book *The East Africa Protectorate* (1905), and of Sir F. D. (afterwards Lord) Lugard, as expressed in *The Dual Mandate in British Tropical Africa* (1922).

In its popular version, transmitted through schools, churches, music-halls, cheap newspapers, and comics and other cheap literature produced for children, racism told the British working class that black people were savages whom British rule was rescuing from heathenism and internecine strife.

Of course, some of these varieties of racism were more 'scientific' than others. What they all had in common was a political function. All of them, in one way or another, justified British rule over black people. And not only over Africans and people of African descent, but over Indians too. Lord Hastings, governor-general of Bengal, said in 1813 of the people over whom he ruled:

> The Hindoo appears a being nearly limited to mere animal functions and even in them indifferent. Their proficiency and skill in the several lines of occupation to which they are restricted, are little more than the dexterity which any animal with similar conformation but with no higher intellect than a dog, an elephant, or a monkey, might be supposed to be capable of attaining.

The different varieties of racism, though they can be analysed for purposes of study into separate strands, as I have done here, were usually jumbled together in the thinking and writing of British politicians, administrators, and propagandists of empire, who found endless ways of demonstrating and asserting that black people were unfit to govern themselves. It is fair to say that all these thinkers and writers, with scarcely an exception, were racists. From the 1870s onwards, in Philip D. Curtin's words, 'virtually every European concerned with imperial theory or imperial administration believed that physical racial appearance was an outward sign of inborn propensities, inclinations, and abilities'.

Until as late as 1942, candidates for the British Colonial Service were required to be of 'pure European descent'. The view that black people were like animals or children — or were indeed 'half animal half children', as the theologian Henry Drummond put it in his book *Tropical Africa* (1888) — and that they therefore needed wise control by white men, was not incompatible with an affectionate though patronising regard for them. A British assistant resident in Nyasaland (now Malawi), writing in 1903, fancied himself to be infinitely wiser than the Africans he lorded it over, but professed also his 'sincere regard' for 'the native': 'I love him somewhat as I love my dog, because he is simple, docile, and cheerful.'

During the period of empire, racism permeated every field of intellectual life in Britain. In no field was its influence more pervasive, or more pernicious, than historiography. Children and young people were taught a version of history which idealised and glamorised Britain and portrayed black people as inferior. Most of the respected names in British nineteenth-century historiography were racists, and most of them reflected in their writings one or other of the central tenets of racist ideology. On the work of these giants towering over the subject there were trained several generations of history students, many of whom went on to teach in schools where the history primers reproduced the same racist mythology. The dominant note in British historiography before 1914, in the words of Eric Williams, was 'justification, encouragement, defence and apology for colonies'. And this justification and defence of colonialism were 'profoundly tainted' with racism. These historians glorified the Teutonic 'race'; they expressed downright British chauvinism; and they displayed contempt for 'inferior races'. Here is just one example from many that could be given.

James Anthony Froude, who became Regius Professor of Modern History at Oxford, has been described as 'creator of that cult of Elizabethan naval heroism which is with us yet in an attenuated form'. Following a visit to the Caribbean, Froude published, in 1888, *The*

English in the West Indies, a book in which he called black people 'children' and 'mere good-natured animals':

> The poor black was a faithful servant as long as he was a slave. As a freeman he is conscious of his inferiority at the bottom of his heart, and would attach himself to a rational white employer with at least as much fidelity as a spaniel. Like the spaniel, too, if he is denied the chance of developing under guidance the better qualities which are in him, he will drift back into a mangy cur. . . .
>
> We have a population to deal with [in the British West Indies], the enormous majority of whom are of an inferior race. . . . Give them independence, and in a few generations they will peel off such civilisation as they have learnt as easily and as willingly as their coats and trousers.

Who can deny that substantially the same views as those expressed by this leading English historian not much more than 100 years ago are still held by many people in Britain, including many people in authority and many people in police uniform?

By 1953 a comparatively small number of black settlers had come to Britain: a few hundred in 1948-50, about 1,000 in 1951, about 2,000 in 1952 and again in 1953. They had come to find work; and they had come on the express invitation of official and semi-official bodies in Britain. Yet their coming led to discussions in the Cabinet.

The content of those discussions was not made public until the release of the relevant Cabinet papers in recent years — though Harold Macmillan had already revealed, in a volume of memoirs published in 1973, that early in 1955 Churchill proposed 'the cry of "Keep Britain White"' as 'a good slogan for the Election which we should soon have to fight without the benefit of his leadership'.

Churchill was in this period the pace-maker of State racism. As early as November 1952 he was asking whether the Post Office was employing 'large numbers of coloured workers. If so, there was some risk that difficult social problems would be created'. Three weeks later the Cabinet asked the home secretary 'to arrange for officials of the Departments concerned to examine the possibilities of preventing any further increase in the number of coloured people seeking employment in this country'. At the same time the chancellor of the exchequer was asked to look into 'the possibility of restricting the number of coloured people obtaining admission to the Civil Service'. And at roughly the same time Churchill was telling officials of the ministry of labour 'that he would not regard unfavourably proposals designed to restrict the entry of coloured workers into Great Britain'. In the same period, too, discussing the settlement of black people in Britain, Churchill told Jamaica's governor, Sir Hugh Foot: 'We would have a magpie society: that would never do.' So there was set up a Cabinet Working Party on Coloured People Seeking Employment in the UK, one of three distinct working parties that gave consideration, in the years 1953-56, to what was seen at the highest level as an 'influx' of black people and a 'coloured invasion'. The Cabinet sought information from the police and the staffs of labour exchanges. The Metropolitan Police reported that 'on the whole coloured people are work-shy and content to live on national assistance and immoral earnings. They are poor workmen. . . They are said to be of low mentality and will only work for short periods'. Police in industrial areas reported that 'coloured people generally are not suited to many forms of work'. Indians and Pakistanis were thought to be 'unscrupulous' and 'not usually a success in work requiring much skill or intellect'. In Newcastle, Glasgow, and Nottingham the police condemned Asians as 'not engaging in any useful or productive work': they 'merely live on the community and produce nothing'. West Africans were described as 'lazy and arrogant': 'They associate with prostitutes and are confirmed gamblers.' The police assured the home secretary that the practice of black men living on the immoral earnings of white women was 'much more widespread than the number of convictions would appear to indicate', and that 'coloured men play a large part in the illicit traffic in Indian hemp'. According to ministry of labour informants, black workers were 'more volatile in temperament than white workers'. They found it hard to accept discipline and were more easily provoked to violence. In the Midlands the view was held by managers of labour exchanges that black workers were 'physically and temperamentally unsuited to the kind of work available in industrial areas'. As for black women,

> it is reported that they are slow mentally and find considerable difficulty in adapting themselves to working conditions in this country. The speed of work in modern factories is said to be quite beyond their capacity. On the other hand they have been found to give fairly reliable service as domestics in hospitals, institutions and private domestic employment.

Some ministers seem to have been specially agitated by the prospect of sexual relations between black people and white people. With evident relief the Committee of Ministers on Colonial Immigrants reported to the Cabinet in June 1956 that 'there seems to be little evidence at present of inter-breeding'. On the other hand,

> 'the indications that there is little inter-breeding at present cannot be projected to justify a forecast for the future. On present evidence a trend towards miscegenation can neither be forecast nor excluded. If such a trend were to occur it would be an important factor.'

Another ministerial concern was the 'political consequences' of a concentration of black voters: 'It is not impossible that, in time, the vote of the coloured population might achieve a significance out of proportion to its size if it were concentrated in, say, half a dozen industrial towns involving twenty or twenty-five constituencies.'

With their minds clouded by this racist mish-mash of immoral earnings, 'inter-breeding', cannabis, and black power, it is scarcely surprising that these ignorant and, on the whole, rather stupid men found black settlement in Britain 'an ominous problem which cannot now be ignored'. And this in spite of the evidence they also had in front of them, in the summer of 1956, that 'up till recently coloured immigrants have had little difficulty in finding work here'; that 'they have not made undue demands on National Assistance'; that 'they have created no particular problem in regard to the Health Service'; that 'they are generally law-abiding'; that, 'except in a few places, their presence has aroused little, if any, public expression of race feeling'. Though they paid lip-service to these facts, the Cabinet still saw the entry of black people as 'an ominous problem'.

Again and again, at a time when black labour was being actively and eagerly recruited by such bodies as London Transport and the British Hotels and Restaurants Association, the Cabinet returned to its secret discussion of how to stop the entry of black people with British passports ('undesirables') while not stopping that of white British subjects from the so-called 'Old Commonwealth': Australia, Canada, New Zealand, and Southern Rhodesia. This was their great dilemma, as they admitted. 'It would obviously be impossible to discriminate openly against coloured people as such in administration or legislation in the field of employment', wrote the home secretary, David Maxwell-Fyfe, in a memorandum dated 30 January 1954. There was, he continued, 'no effective means of stopping this influx' without giving immigration officers authority to refuse leave to land. And there could be no question of seeking such power to deal only with coloured people: it would have to be a power which could be exercised in relation to any British subject from overseas. Immigration control, said his successor Gwilym Lloyd-George ten months later, 'would have to be imposed on all British subjects alike', though it would be made to operate 'with the minimum of inconvenience' to those of them whose skins happened to be white. Viscount Swinton, secretary of state for Commonwealth relations, was not convinced that legislation 'should be non-discriminatory in form'. 'We shall welcome', he wrote in a November 1954 memorandum, 'the comparatively few good young Canadians or New Zealanders who wish to work here, while restricting an excessive number of West Indians.' Other Commonwealth countries had this problem, he observed, and in some cases their legislation was non-discriminatory in form while their administration was discriminatory in practice — and 'we too shall have to discriminate in practice'. In a later memorandum (June 1955) Swinton wrote of the 'large and continuing influx of coloured persons into this country'. There was no means of controlling this 'influx' without legislation. If such legislation extended to all British subjects without discrimination, some 'administrative easements' in favour of white immigrants would be needed. The cunning solution to the dilemma was a proposed system of work permits, which would be granted only to skilled workers. A prospective employer would have to seek permission for the entry of a named immigrant. This, it was thought, would both exclude almost all black immigrants and frustrate any accusations of discrimination on the ground of colour. So assurances could readily be given that the policy was an impartial one. Immigration officials would have complete discretion to refuse entry to those whom they regarded as 'undesirables'. And the new regulations would be rigorously applied only at ports where immigrants from the Caribbean normally arrived.

Thus, in the words of Edward Pilkington, author of *Beyond the Mother Country: West Indians and the Notting Hill White Riots* (1988) 'by 1956 a full blue-print already existed for a racially discriminatory system of immigration controls'. This blue-print was put into effect by the notorious Commonwealth Immigrants Act of 1962, the first in that long shameful series of legislative measures that have made scarcely concealed racist discrimination part of British law. The 1962 act restricted the admission of Commonwealth immigrants to those who had been issued with employment vouchers. It made serious inroads into the civil rights of black British citizens whose passports had been issued outside the United Kingdom. And it officially equated black skin with second-class citizenship. The unspoken assumption of the 1962 Act was the premise on which all the Cabinet discussions in the 1950s had been based: that the problem wasn't white racism, but the presence of black people in Britain. In 1962 racism was enshrined in British law for the first time. The Act's intention and effect were to restrict the entry of black people, though it was claimed that this restriction wasn't particularly aimed at people who weren't white.

From that 1962 Act everything else has flowed. Concession after concession has been made to racism. So, a generation later, we live in a racist society, which treats black people born in Britain as second-class citizens in the country of their birth. All strata of our society are infected, one way or another, with racist poison. We have had a prime minister who feared 'that this country might be rather swamped by people with a different culture'. We have had a junior minister in charge of ethnic monitoring in unemployment benefit offices who spoke of black people's countries of origin as 'Bongo Bongo Land'. We have had a senior adviser on 'race relations' at the Home Office who, at a conference of the Police Federation, referred to black people as 'nig nogs'. We have had an operational chief of the Metropolitan Police's no. 6 area in west London who, discussing street signs for the 1986 Notting Hill carnival, said the signs should read: 'Coons go home.' We had not long ago a Metropolitan Police commissioner who told an American journalist that 'in the Jamaicans, you have people who are constitutionally disorderly. . . . It's simply in their make-up. They are constitutionally disposed to be anti-authority'.

We have in fact a police force that is racist from top to bottom, in belief and behaviour alike. This was clearly shown by the Policy Studies Institute report on the Metropolitan Police, published in 1983. Racist talk and racial prejudice, said this report, are 'expected, accepted and even fashionable'; 'one criterion that police officers use for stopping people, especially in areas of relatively low ethnic concentration, is that they are black'; 'police officers tend to make a crude equation between crime and black people, to assume that suspects are black and to justify stopping people in these terms'; 'to a considerable extent, police hostility towards people of West Indian origin is connected with the belief that they are rootless, alienated, poor, unable to cope and deviant in various ways'; police officers freely use such racist terms as 'coons', 'niggers', 'satchies', 'sooties', 'spades', 'monkeys', 'spooks', and 'Pakis'; 'we cannot produce examples of police officers objecting to racialist language'; 'apart from these casually abusive references, there is a vein of deliberately hostile and bitter comment on black people by police officers'; 'hostility to black people is linked, in the minds of these police officers, with racialist theories, right wing politics, fear of violence and disorder caused by black people, a psychological need for retribution and the view that violent retribution is legitimate'. And this damning report, the most extensive study of the Metropolitan Police ever carried out, concluded that 'the level of racial prejudice in the Force is cause for serious concern'.

Encouraged by State racism and police racism, fascist gangs have in recent years stepped up their attacks on black people. Children are shot at with airgun pellets; meat cleavers, Stanley knives, and fire-bombs are used; pensioners, students, shopkeepers, and infants are among the victims.

Black people born in Britain are a permanent part of British society. They are here to stay. They will not put up with State racism, police racism, and racist harassment by fascist gangs. With ever-increasing determination they are defending themselves, their children, their homes, and their communities. In this they have the active support of all white people who have begun to understand the painful lessons, the painful truths, taught by black history.

5

Resistance

Throughout these lectures I've been seeking to combat a whole series of myths that British historians and other apologists for empire have sought to foster, about the essential altruism and benevolence of British imperial rule. Now I want to challenge yet another myth of empire: the idea that, on the whole, black people responded to British rule with, at worst, passive resignation; with, at best, gratitude.

This is not the least false or the least pernicious of these myths which are still being fostered. Take a look, for instance at the *History of the British West Indies* (1954), by Sir Alan Burns, a book which is still, I think, a standard text. 'The . . . Negro population', wrote Sir Alan, 'during the centuries of slavery, had little to do, save indirectly, with the shaping of events.' The corresponding myth in relation to the Indian sub-continent tells us that the population enjoyed a pax Britannica, a 'British peace', during the rule of the East India Company and the direct British rule that followed it. Before the British came, and after they left, disorder, anarchy, unrest, and bloodshed; but under the Union Jack a miraculous peace. Well, it simply wasn't true in India, and it wasn't true in the British Caribbean either.

Nowhere within the British Empire, in fact, were black people passive victims. On the contrary, they were everywhere active resisters. Far from being docile, they resisted slavery and colonialism in every way open to them. Their resistance took a myriad different forms, both individual and collective. It ranged from a watchful and waiting pretence of acceptance — a subtle if elementary form of individual resistance to slavery — right up to large-scale mass uprisings and national liberation movements. Throughout the Caribbean, as long as slavery lasted, resistance was the norm and not the exception. The slaves did as little work as possible, a form of resistance interpreted by stupid or unimaginative observers as laziness. They frequently 'lost' or damaged their working tools. They feigned illness, inflicted injuries on themselves, sometimes killed themselves either individually or in groups — and this wasn't a cry of despair, but a cry of defiance. Cultural resistance took the shape of songs and dances either blisteringly satirising the planters and their families or else preparing the slaves for rebellion — as did, for instance, the kalinda of Trinidad and Dominica and elsewhere, a stick-fighting dance that no doubt derives from African dances teaching young men the martial arts. Vast numbers of slaves resisted by running away: in Jamaica in the 1820s, the decade before emancipation, there were more runaways than ever before. In revenge for acts of cruelty, slaves sometimes beat planters and overseers to death or poisoned them. A threat, in politics as in chess, is often more powerful than its execution; and the ever-present threat of rebellion cost the slaves less than actual revolt and kept the planters in a state of perpetual fear. But serious uprisings were far more frequent than historians have, until quite recently, been prepared to acknowledge.

The indispensable book on slave rebellions in the British West Indies is *Testing the Chains* (1982) by Michael Craton, who lists and describes no fewer than 75 such rebellions between the years 1638 and 1837 — that is, roughly one every two-and-a-half years. All but 17 of these rebellions involved at least hundreds of slaves and 22 involved thousands or many thousands. Another scholar, Orlando Patterson, has pointed out that during Jamaica's 180 years of slavery under British rule 'hardly a decade went by without a serious, large-scale revolt threatening the entire system'.

There obviously isn't time for me tonight to do more than mention a few of these rebellions, which were generally put down by the British authorities with the utmost ferocity and cruelty. It is highly instructive to discover that in one of the earliest of them, which took place in Barbados in 1683, leaflets were distributed handwritten in English, already the lingua franca of Africans from different ethnic groups. One of these leaflets is preserved in the Public Record Office, where anybody can go to inspect it and marvel at it. It begins 'Brothers', and says 'wee have most of all Countreyes of our Side' — in other words, that Africans of different ethnic groups were united in the struggle. Craton reproduces this astonishing leaflet in his book, and it destroys three myths at the same time: the myth that the slaves were passive victims; the myth that they were all illiterate; and the myth that 'modern' methods of propaganda and agitation didn't emerge until the nineteenth century. I have had British-born children of twelve and thirteen, of Afro-Caribbean descent, say to me that they detest being reminded that they are the descendants of slaves; that this for them is a matter of shame and humiliation. All the more reason to teach them the historical truth that they are the descendants of freedom fighters, who fought tenaciously against their oppressors with remarkable courage and no less remarkable sophistication.

So well did they fight that in Jamaica, in the eighteenth century, the British authorities were forced more than once to sue for peace and to conclude treaties with the runaway slaves, or maroons, thousands of whom had been waging guerrilla warfare all over the island. These treaties led to the establishment of what nowadays we would call 'liberated areas', though in order to gain their own freedom the maroons undertook to perform policing duties against future runaways and rebels. One of the outstanding maroon leaders in Jamaica was a redoubtable woman called Nanny, who gave her name to Nanny Town in the Blue Mountains. Enslaved black women were strong. They had to be. And Nanny was one of the strongest of them. All sorts of stories are still told about her — for instance, that she used to catch British cannon-balls in her buttocks and fart them back at the enemy. When stories like this are found in the oral tradition after more than 200 years, having been passed on from generation to generation, we may be sure that we are in the presence of a quite outstanding personality, a quite outstanding leader.

It makes a lot of sense to divide the slave rebellions in the British Caribbean into two periods: before and after the great Haitian revolution that began in 1791. What happened in Haiti had an enormous influence on political consciousness and struggle everywhere else in the Caribbean, and not least in the British-held islands and territories. The key book on the Haiti events is *The Black Jacobins* (1938) by C. L. R. James, which still holds its place as a classic of black historiography. It is a model of historical research and clarity of presentation, not least in what it has to teach us about the role of the masses in history and about what happens when they erupt on to the historical scene. (And I would remind you that when he researched, wrote, and published that book, C. L. R. James was a Trotskyist, an adherent of the Fourth International.) James showed how the Haitian masses seized the banner of liberty, equality, and fraternity raised by the French bourgeois-democratic revolution, and surged forward under that banner to unleash the greatest slave revolt in human history. They did away with slavery and won national independence. Not least important, they provided a powerful example to the nascent working-class movement in Europe, as well as to slaves elsewhere in the Caribbean.

The Haitian revolution sent a shudder of terror through the British plantocracy in the Caribbean, and within four years 7,000 slaves in Grenada, under a battle flag with the slogan '*Liberté, égalité ou la mort*' ('Freedom, equality or death'), and wearing tricolour cockades and caps of liberty, had set up their own revolutionary government, so that, in Craton's words, 'at the beginning of 1796 Grenada was a black republic under arms, with St George's the single imperial enclave'. The rebels were not defeated until they were outnumbered ten to one.

There is time only to mention the uprising of 1796-97 in St Lucia, the so-called Brigands' War, when the slaves went into battle, and many to the scaffold, shouting '*Vive la république!*' ('Long live the republic!'); the Second Maroon War in Dominica (1809-14); the 1816 revolt in Barbados, led by, amongst others, a woman slave called Nanny Grigg; the 1823 revolt in Demerara; the 1823 revolt, known as the Argyle War, in Jamaica; and the climax of slave rebellions in the British Caribbean, the mass uprising in Jamaica in 1831-32, the so-called Baptist War, which mobilized 60,000 slaves over an area of 750 square miles and was without doubt one of the principal factors that led to the abolition of slavery in 1833.

For 200 years the slaves tied down large numbers of British troops in costly and demoralising operations. They caused endless trouble to planters and governors; they levied a huge tax on the plantation economy, in terms of crops and equipment destroyed. They made a massive cumulative contribution to emancipation. They proved themselves to be the most dynamic and powerful social force in the colonies. And their ceaseless resistance was unquestionably the most important single factor in their emancipation.

Black resistance to British rule in the Caribbean continued in the century following emancipation. Here again it is helpful to divide this period into two. Before the emergence of the industrial working class in the Caribbean the resistance movement was largely, though not exclusively, a question of peasant insurrections. There were 21 major rebellions in the British Caribbean between 1841 and 1905: six in Jamaica; five in British Guiana; four in Trinidad; two in Dominica; and one each in Barbados, British Honduras (now Belize), Montserrat, and

St Kitts. Of these the most important was the 1865 rebellion in Jamaica, led by the peasant smallholder and Baptist preacher Paul Bogle, which was put down with the utmost brutality by Governor Edward Eyre, whom I mentioned in the previous lecture. In a month-long reign of terror he shot down or executed 439 people; subjected 600 people, including pregnant women, to the most barbaric floggings; and wantonly destroyed 1,000 houses. Yet the 1865 uprising in Jamaica hardly figures at all in British history books.

With the 1905 riots in British Guiana we come to a new period, when the industrial working class has entered the arena as an independent force with its own demands. This class became the backbone of the anti-imperialist struggle in the British Caribbean. There were two peak periods in the struggle. The first began towards the end of World War I, with strike movements in Trinidad, Tobago, British Honduras, Jamaica, Grenada, and elsewhere. The second peak period was the 1930s, when there was a revolutionary upsurge throughout the Caribbean, beginning with a revolt by workers and the unemployed in British Honduras in 1934, and culminating in mass uprisings in Trinidad in 1937, Barbados in the same year, and Jamaica in 1938. I'm bound to say I find it strange that no one in Britain, so far as I am aware, saw fit in 1988 to organise any sort of commemoration of the fiftieth anniversary of those events, when every British governor in the Caribbean screamed for warships, marines, and the Royal Air Force, and 46 people were killed, 429 were wounded, when thousands were thrown in jail. For three months in 1938 Jamaica's workers and peasants downed tools, marched in demonstrations, looted shops, cut telephone wires, put up road-blocks, tore down bridges, burnt crops, besieged the rich in their houses, and, armed only with sticks and stones, fought back with the utmost courage against armed police and troops. They shook the whole British colonial system to its foundations, so that it was never to be the same again. But it is as if these events had never happened. Nobody wants to remember them. And yet they led to the appointment of the Moyne Commission, which investigated social conditions throughout the British West Indies and submitted its report at the end of 1939 (but the report gave such a grim account of the British Empire's neglected backwater that its publication was held up for five-and-a-half years, until World War II was over). Ultimately the uprisings of the 1930s led to British imperialism deciding, at long last, to drop these hot potatoes of colonies whose populations had proved with their blood that they would not submit to continued British rule.

It's hardly possible in the time available to do justice to the resistance of the peoples of the Indian sub-continent to British rule between 1765 and 1946 — nearly 200 years of virtually unbroken resistance, from the Sannyasi uprising of 1772-74 to the mutiny by sailors of the Royal Indian Navy which began on 18 February 1946; and on the very next day the British government announced that it was sending a Cabinet Mission to India to begin the negotiations that were to lead to independence in 1947. Again, it was the struggle of the Indian workers and peasants that won them independence. The two highlights of that struggle were the so-called 'Mutiny' — in fact a national rising — in 1857-58, which it would take a whole lecture, or rather a series of lectures, to discuss adequately, and in which a prominent part was played by a 23-year-old woman, Laxmi Bai, Rani of Jhansi, who was killed while fighting, sword in hand, at the head of 1,500 men; and the great national uprising of 1942-43, foully betrayed by the Indian Stalinists, in which between 10,000 and 15,000 freedom fighters were killed. There were mass attacks on government buildings; prisons were stormed and prisoners set free; the insurgents operated an anti-government radio station in Bombay; and countless unarmed demonstrators were shot dead, including a 73-year-old woman, Matangini Hazra, who led a demonstration in the Bengal town of Midnapore. British repression was utterly ruthless. Over 60,000 people were arrested, and many of them were tortured in custody. And the Royal Air Force machine-gunned railwaymen and villagers: in five months 348 people were killed in air raids in the Calcutta area and elsewhere. But, though it was crushed by the full weight of British arms, this great movement undoubtedly paved the way for Indian independence four years later.

6

Black radicals in the early British working-class movement

Let's begin this final lecture with some observations by John Major, taken from a news item in the *Guardian* of 26 September 1991, according to which our prime minister 'spoke out . . . about racial prejudice in Britain and declared his personal commitment to eradicate it'. The report went on:

> Mr Major spoke of his roots in Brixton and named some of the personalities of the historical black community in Britain — Ira Aldridge, the Victorian [*sic*] actor, Mary Seacole, who nursed in the Crimea, Samuel Taylor Coleridge [*sic*], the composer and Sir Learie Constantine the West Indian cricketer who also became the first black peer.

Mr Major was addressing black graduates attending a prize-giving in the City of London. Many of them no doubt knew that Ira Aldridge made his name as an actor of genius long before Queen Victoria ascended the throne in 1837; that he was subjected by many London critics to a virulently racist campaign, *The Times*, for instance, claiming that it was impossible for him to speak English properly 'owing to the shape of his lips', and the *Athenæum* protesting, 'in the name of propriety and decency', against a white actress being 'pawed about' on the stage by a black man; that the West End stage boycotted him for years; and that he found on the Continent, above all in Russia, the recognition largely denied him here in Britain. Mr Major's audience could also have told him, no doubt, that Samuel Taylor Coleridge was

a white English poet and that the Anglo-African composer Mr Major
or his speech-writer had in mind was called Samuel Coleridge-Taylor.
They might have added that Learie Constantine was not merely 'the'
West Indian cricketer but one of the greatest all-rounders in the game's
history, and that in 1944 he won a celebrated court action for breach
of contract after a leading London hotel refused him admittance
because, as the hotel manageress delicately put it, 'he is a nigger'.

These however are minor points compared with Mr Major's choice
of four 'safe', 'respectable', middle-class names to drop before his
graduate audience, and his striking omission of four other names, clearly
not so 'safe' and rather less 'respectable', but of at least as much
significance in the history of the British black community, and of great
significance in the history of the British working-class movement:
Olaudah Equiano, William Davidson, Robert Wedderburn, and
William Cuffay.

By the middle of the eighteenth century there was in Britain a black
population of at least 10,000, most of them slave-servants brought here
by absentee West India planters as part of their household retinues.
Between about 1740 and about 1790 these black slaves emancipated
themselves as individuals by running away from their masters and
mistresses. By this long-drawn-out process of self-emancipation, which
has been studied in detail by the Canadian historian Douglas Lorimer,
they made a decisive contribution to the English tradition of love of
liberty and hatred of slavery. Their achievement constituted the first
victory of the abolitionist movement in Britain, and did much to ensure
the centrality of anti-slavery to the thinking and the demands of the
emerging working-class radical movement in this country in the 1790s.
And in this long-drawn-out process of self-emancipation black slaves in
Britain had reliable allies in London's working people: the so-called
'Mob'. Listen to Sir John Fielding, London's 'Blind Beak', the
magistrate (and half-brother of the novelist Henry Fielding), writing in
1768, in a book called *Extracts from such of the penal laws, as Particularly
relate to the Peace and Good Order of this metropolis*. This is an
extraordinary passage, and it's well worth quoting at length. Sir John
Fielding is writing about black people in London in 1768:

> They no sooner arrive here, than they put themselves on a Footing with
> other Servants, become intoxicated with Liberty, grow refractory, and
> . . . begin to expect Wages. . . . A great Number of black Men and

Women . . . have made themselves so troublesome and dangerous to the Families who brought them over as to get themselves discharged; these enter into Societies, and make it their business to corrupt and dissatisfy the Mind of every fresh black Servant that comes to *England*. . . . It gets the Mob on their Side, and makes it not only difficult but dangerous to the Proprietor of these Slaves to recover the Possession of them, when once they are spirited away. . . . There is great Reason to fear that those Blacks who have been sent back to the Plantations, after they have lived some Time in a Country of Liberty, where they have learnt to write and read, been acquainted with the Use, and entrusted with the Care[,] of Arms, have been the Occasion of those Insurrections that have lately caused and threatened such Mischiefs and Dangers to the Inhabitants of, and Planters in[,] the Islands in the *West-Indies*; it is therefore to be hoped that these Gentlemen will be extremely cautious for the future, how they bring Blacks to *England*. . . . They no sooner come over, but the Sweets of Liberty and the Conversation with free Men and Christians, enlarge their Minds, and . . . make them restless, prompt to conceive, and alert to execute[,] the blackest Conspiracies against their Governors and Masters.

In this remarkable passage we are hearing the authentic voice of the British governing and 'master' class. This passage tells us several very interesting things. It tells us that black people in Britain were organised into 'Societies'. It suggests that there were links between those organisations and the resistance movement in the Caribbean. And it tells us that the black slaves in Britain who emancipated themselves by running away had allies: that they had 'the Mob on their Side'.

Now, who were the 'Mob'? They were the working people of London, the pre-industrial craftsmen and labourers, who periodically poured into the streets to riot against their rulers and in defence of liberty. Black people were part of that 'Mob', and in 1780 a black woman called Charlotte Gardener was hanged on Tower Hill for her part in the Gordon Riots of that year. London's working people saw black people as fellow-victims of their own enemies, as fellow-fighters against a system that degraded poor whites and poor blacks alike. And, with the help of London's working people, London was in the second half of the eighteenth century a centre of black resistance.

It is hard to over-estimate the contribution made by the anti-slavery struggle both in the Caribbean and here in Britain to the nascent working-class movement. Ablitionism was shamefully slow to develop in Britain. The slave trade was carried on for more than a hundred years before a movement to abolish it emerged. And, when this movement did finally emerge, it was at first a middle-class movement. By 1787 only about five or six anti-slavery books had been published in England. Then a black man living in London, a former slave, published the most powerful such book yet to appear: *Thoughts and sentiments on the evil and wicked traffic of the slavery and commerce of the human species.* The author of that book was a former slave called Ottobah Cugoano, who took the name John Steuart. He was a Fante from what is today called Ghana. Two years later Cugoano's friend Olaudah Equiano, otherwise known as Gustavus Vassa, and also a former slave, published his autobiography, another powerful trumpet-blast against slavery: *The Interesting Narrative of the Life of Olaudah Equiano, or Gustavus Vassa, the African.* This highly influential book went through eight British editions in its author's lifetime and six more in the 22 years after his death. Equiano, one of the most outstanding black people who has ever lived in Britain, was an Igbo from what is now Nigeria. Among his friends was a young Scottish shoemaker called Thomas Hardy, who was chief founder and first secretary of the London Corresponding Society, the strongest of Britain's radical working-class organisations in the 1790s. And there is preserved in the Public Record Office a letter from Equiano to Hardy which makes it clear, not only that Hardy and his comrades in the LCS had put the struggle against slavery as one of their central tasks and preoccupations, but also that Equiano had become a member of the LCS. Writing from Edinburgh, where he was addressing public meetings and selling copies of his book, Equiano wrote: 'My best Respect to my fellow members of your society. I hope they do yet increase.' Not only did Equiano join the LCS; on his speaking-tours all over the British Isles, he sent to Hardy the names and addresses of what today we would call his 'contacts': people he met who supported the campaign for the abolition of the slave trade and with whom Hardy might usefully get in touch as possible supporters of the radical movement.

Here we have a two-pronged tradition: black people playing a part in the emerging British radical working-class movement, and British workers, especially after the Haitian revolution, making the abolition of slavery one of their central aims. Here in 1792, many years before Marx declared that labour in a white skin could not be emancipated while labour in a black skin was branded, we find Thomas Hardy writing to a Sheffield clergyman:

Hearing from Gustavus Vassa that you are a zealous friend for the

Abolition of that accursed traffick denominated the Slave Trade I inferred from that that you was a friend to freedom on the broad basis of the Rights of Man for I am pretty perswaded that no Man who is an advocate from principle for liberty for a Black Man but will strenuously promote and support the rights of a White Man & vice versa.

When Sheffield radicals organised a big mass meeting in 1794, attended by thousands of artisan cutlers, a unanimous resolution called for the emancipation of black slaves and the ending of the slave trade: 'Its Abolition', declared this resolution, '. . . will avenge . . . ages of wrongs done to our Negro Brethren.' And John Thelwall of the London Corresponding Society, the English radical most feared by the government of the day, addressing huge meetings in London and the provinces in 1794 and 1795, directly linked the struggle against slavery with the struggle against a corrupt ruling class at home. 'If we would dispense justice to our distant colonies,' he declared, 'we must begin by rooting out from the centre the corruption by which that cruelty and injustice is countenanced and defended.'

This tradition was carried forward in the first half of the nineteenth century by three black radicals in Britain. If you go to the Public Record Office in Kew you will find boxes of documents containing reports of police spies and *agents provocateurs* in the radical working-class movement in the Regency period, and you will find preserved in one of those boxes a secret list of 33 'leadeing Reformers' compiled for the home secretary from police reports in 1819. (You will also find the actual reports that sent brave men to the gallows; and handling those documents will make you shudder with horror, particularly when you remember that this vile system of spying on the working-class movement continues to this day, though nowadays it takes much more sophisticated forms.) Well, this list of 33 leading radicals that was put before the home secretary in 1819 has a little cross against two of the names, and at the bottom of the page there is a little cross again, and a note saying 'Black Man'. The two names are those of William Davidson and Robert Wedderburn, both of whom had been born in Jamaica, and both of whom were members of revolutionary socialist organisations in the troubled years 1817-20.

Davidson, a cabinet-maker by trade, who was known as 'Black Davidson' and had recently been elected secretary of the newly formed shoemakers' trade union, was hanged on 1 May 1820, with four of his white comrades, for their part in what became known as the the Cato Street conspiracy. These were men burning with indignation over the

Peterloo massacre the previous year, when an unarmed and peaceful demonstration of Manchester cotton-spinners and their wives and children had been savagely attacked by the Yeomanry, who were the Manchester manufacturers and merchants on horseback. Eleven people, including two women and a child, had been killed by sabre-cuts, and about 420 others, over 100 of them women and girls, had been hurt. 'Black Davidson' and his comrades decided to execute the Cabinet of tyrants who had been responsible for that crime. They agreed to a plan suggested to them by a police spy called George Edwards, who betrayed them to the authorities.

Robert Wedderburn, a tailor, was a member of another revolutionary socialist group in London. His organisation held a debate in 1819 on whether a slave had the right to kill a master. This question 'was decided in Favor of the Slave without a dissenting Voice, by a numerous and enlightened Assembly, who exultingly expressed their Desire of hearing of another sable Nation freeing itself by the Dagger from the base Tyranny of their Christian Masters'; indeed, 'Several Gentlemen declared their readiness to assist them'. This led the authorities to prosecute Wedderburn for sedition and blasphemy, and he was jailed more than once for one or other of these crimes. It was Wedderburn who sent the first known revolutionary propaganda from Britain to the Caribbean, in the shape of a journal called *The Axe Laid to the Root, or a Fatal Blow to Oppressors, being an address to the Planters and Negroes of the Island of Jamaica*. And in this extraordinary document, which caused consternation in the planters' assembly in Jamaica, Wedderburn expressed his vision of a simultaneous revolution of the white poor in Europe and the black slaves in the Caribbean — in 1817, a year before Karl Marx was born! *The Axe Laid to the Root* contains these ringing words: 'I am a West-Indian, a lover of liberty, and would dishonour human nature if I did not shew myself a friend to the liberty of others.' Wedderburn also, by the way, had contacts among the Irish community in London, who assured him that they would join the uprising when it began.

The last of the three black British radicals of the nineteenth century that I want to glance at is William Cuffay, who was born in 1788 in Chatham, the son of an former slave from St Kitts, and who became a tailor. He also became one of the leaders of the Chartist movement in London, which *The Times* referred to as 'the black man and his party'. (Cuffay wasn't, by the way, the only black person who played an active part in London Chartism. Two of the leaders of a demonstration in Camberwell in 1848 were described in the press as 'men of colour': they were two seafarers called David Anthony Duffy and Benjamin Prophitt; Duffy was transported for seven years, Prophitt for fourteen.) Cuffay also seems to have had close contacts with the Irish community in London. Following the fiasco of the 1848 Kennington Common demonstration, Cuffay was found guilty, on the evidence of two spies in the pay of the Metropolitan Police, of 'levying war on Queen Victoria'. He was transported for life to Tasmania, where he died in 1870, aged 82.

These black radicals helped to secure for our generation the civil liberties we enjoy and cherish and must defend: freedom of speech, freedom of assembly, freedom to organise, freedom to protest and demonstrate. It must never be forgotten that the British ruling class did not hand those civil liberties to the working class on a plate. The working class had to struggle for them, and that struggle was long, hard, and bitter. Our civil liberties were won in struggle by men and women who had the guts to endure vilification, arrest, imprisonment, and transportation, and face even the prospect of execution. And among those courageous men and women of our great-great-grandfathers' generation were the African Olaudah Equiano and those three men of African descent: William Davidson, Robert Wedderburn, and William Cuffay. These four black men did much to help build our British labour movement. Let us honour their tradition. And let us do all we can to make sure that their tradition and their contribution are never forgotten.

Index

abolitionist movement, 9, 46-8
absentee planters, 15, 46
Africa and Africans, 7, 9, 12, 13, 14, 16, 17, 18, 28, 32, 34, 40, 51
Aldridge, Ira, 45
Anglo-Saxonism, 30-1
Anthropological Society of London, 30
anthropology, 30
Arkwright, Sir Richard, 22
Arnold, Thomas, 31
Asians in Britain, 34
assiento, 14, 18, 19
Athenæum, 45
Australia, 35
Axe Laid to the Root, The, 50

Bai, Laxmi, 44
Bank of England, 16
banking system, 16
Barbados, 12, 17; resistance, 40, 42, 43; 1816 revolt, 42; 1937 uprising, 43
Barclays Bank, 16
Behar, 20
Belize, *see* British Honduras
Benares, 22
Bengal, 7, 19, 20, 21, 23, 24, 25, 31, 44
Benin, 9
Birmingham, 12, 13
black history and white people, 5-10
Black Jacobins, The (1938), 41
Board of Trade, 29
Bogle, Paul, 43
Bombay, 22, 44
Bristol, 9, 12, 13
Britain: black presence, 5-6, 7, 26, 46ff; labour movement, 8, 9, 46-51; post-war black settlement, 26, 33ff; self-emancipation of black slaves, 46-7
British Empire, 7-8, 11, 25, 26, 29-30, 39, 43
British Guiana, 17; resistance, 42, 43; 1905 riots, 43
British Honduras, 43; strike movement, 43; 1934 revolt, 43
British Hotels and Restaurants Association, 35
Bulwer-Lytton, Sir Edward (*afterwards* first Baron Lytton), 31
Burns, Sir Alan, 39

Cabinet discussions on black settlement in Britain (1952-56), 33-6
Cabinet Working Party on Coloured People Seeking Employment in the UK, 34
Calcutta, 22, 44
Camberwell, 50
Cambridge History of the British Empire, 15
Canada, 35
Capital, 11-12
Cardiff, 8
Caribbean, 7, 11, 17, 28, 29, 32, 39, 50; anti-imperialist struggle, 43ff; Moyne Commission, 43; resistance in, 39ff, 47; revolutionary upsurge (1930s), 43; *see also under names of islands and territories*
Carlyle, Thomas, 30, 31
Cato Street conspiracy, 49-50
Charles II, King, 13
Chartism, 50
Chatham, 50
child labour in Britain, 17-18
China, 20
Churchill, Sir Winston, 11, 34
civil liberties, 51
Civil Service, 33
Clarkson, Thomas, 9
Clive, Robert, 19, 21-2
coal industry, 15
Coleridge, Samuel Taylor, 45
Coleridge-Taylor, Samuel, 46
Colonial Service, British, 32
commission agents, 12
Committee of Ministers on Colonial